Welcome!

• • • • • • • • • • • • • •

a personal guide to
hosting on Airbnb

Roxanne Lawrence
2014 and 2015 Airbnb
Superhost Award Winner!

©2015 Published by Violet Stone Press

Welcome!
A Personal Guide to
Hosting on Airbnb®

© 2015 by Roxanne V. Lawrence

Published by:
Violet Stone Press
1379 W. Park Western Ave.
Suite 309
San Pedro, CA 90732
VioletStonePress@gmail.com

First Printing, 2015

Printed in the United State of America

ISBN: 978-1516807048

Contents

Contents

Dedication

This personal guide to hosting with Airbnb® is dedicated to our very first guest, Russell C. Smith, all those who have come after him, and all those we have yet to meet!

It is also dedicated to the new sharing and caring economy created in part by everyone taking the plunge by hosting or staying at an Airbnb®!

I wish to acknowledge my sister, Michelle Lawrence, my daughter, Shannon Paul, my book guru, Mike Rounds and my graphic designer/editor, Leslie Sears for their constant love, support and patience while writing this guide. I am grateful!

Foreword

Can you take a $20 bill and turn it into thousands????

Guess what? YOU CAN!!

By following our simple and proven framework and guidelines—YOU can take that unused space in your home and turn it into a profitable and fun experience hosting guests using Airbnb® (or other sites)!

Two years ago, my sister Michelle and I bought a home with an apartment over the garage. Our intention was to live in the house and use the apartment as a rental with a full-time tenant.

As Michelle is a realtor in the area, we knew we could probably get a decent rental price and have a tenant there for an entire year.

But since the apartment's water, gas and electric service are on our bill, we'd be paying their utilities; plus seeing their friends come and go, and contending with the likelihood of the occasional rowdy party. That didn't sound like a lot of fun!

Since the apartment is literally in our backyard, another option presented itself to us: having our own bed and breakfast business.

Between the two of us, we have travelled to almost all seven continents, seen the midnight sun, haggled in bazaars, had our fortunes told in Angkor Wat, sailed to Africa, been chased by kangaroos, and even lived in Las Vegas!

We have stayed in the gamut of accommodations from sweaty youth hostels to a few Four Seasons and Ritz Carltons! We figured we knew a thing or two about what it takes to create a good lodging experience.

By turning our apartment into a B & B, we could control the calendar, block it out for friends to stay, leave it vacant when we wanted some privacy, and rent it at other times to make some money.

We asked questions of people who were doing the hosting gig already but no one seemed to have a checklist or any streamlined instructions to pass on to us. We liked what Airbnb® had to offer, so we signed up and gleaned what we could from their website.

Like so many things in life, when something doesn't exist, you have to create it, so we created our own guide and checklists. Once we got it up and going, our B & B has been super successful. We were even awarded the Airbnb® SUPERHOST AWARD in 2014 and 2015!

Many of our friends have empty rooms in their homes and said if only there was an easily followed guide or framework then they would host too. So here it is: Frameworks, Guide, and Checklists to turn your spare room into a home business! Try it and see if it is for you!

Enjoy the journey and a million thank yous to the founders of Airbnb®! You guys rock!!!

About the Author

Roxanne Lawrence is a graduate of the University of Southern California, former Air Force Intelligence Officer, and a member of the International Longshore and Warehouse Union for over 27 years.

Currently residing in the port town of San Pedro, south of Los Angeles, she has lived in Europe, Asia, and Las Vegas.

Since her first trip to Europe and the Middle East at age 12, she has camped in tents in the Sahara desert, cruised the Tasman Sea and danced the mambo in Havana.

She received the Airbnb® SuperHost Award in 2014 and 2015 and spreads her joy of hosting to her guests and future hosts through this personal guide.

Introduction

What is Airbnb®?

Airbnb® is a website where you will find over 1,000,000 listings of places to stay in 33,000 cities and 192 countries.

According to their figures, over 25 million guests have stayed in Airbnb®s, and there are over 600 castles listed in the inventory!

Airbnb® recently announced it was launching in Cuba with over 1,000 listings.

Beyond being a significant milestone in the normalization of relations with Cuba and a sign of pent up demand for travel, this is a significant milestone for the industry.

Founded in 2008 and headquartered in San Francisco, CA, Airbnb® is a privately owned company.

A web-based community marketplace where guests can book accommodations from hosts, it connects people who have space to spare with those seeking lodging.

Users of the site must register and create a personal online profile.

Every property is associated with a host whose profile includes recommendations by other users, reviews by previous guests, as well as a response rating and private messaging system.

The site can be used worldwide and there is an Airbnb® mobile app.

All payment is through the website and once a reservation is completed, both host and guest can review each other to build a reputation in the community.

Chapter 1 - Deciding if becoming a host on Airbnb® is for you!

Can you be a host on Airbnb®? The answer, according to their website, is that almost anyone can be a host, and it is free to sign up! With so many diverse places to stay, you can list your space in almost any location worldwide.

Check the website to see how you will describe your space and the many room types available to list. My daughter recently stayed in a jungle bungalow cottage on a papaya farm in Hawaii, so add it to the list of pretty creative and non-traditional places to lay your head on Airbnb®.

My parents stayed in not one, but two castles in Europe, another friend rents out his yacht in LA Harbor. Friends have stayed in Airstream trailers, while another friend ended up being hosted by royalty in Paris!

Don't think you can't host just because you don't have an extra bedroom. You may have some space where someone can spend some fun and quality time.

With the ability to rent out almost anything, individuals can now capitalize on items (rooms, homes) that would otherwise not be in use.

Due to increases in internet accessibility, online social networking, mobile technology, apps, and location based services, the peer-to-peer on-line marketplace is booming.

Today the host is the brand, and it is changing the hospitality business, while pumping money into the local, not corporate, economy. The new travel entrepreneurs are providing the three things travelers seek: location, value, and service.

This results in a sharing and caring economy, accomplished through Airbnb® by allowing its users to trustfully book and review their stays. Coupled with the general apathy and mediocrity of the big brand hotels, this has brought Airbnb® huge success.

As we considered turning our apartment into a B & B, there were many pros and cons for our situation, and luckily the pros won out.

The first issue dealt with the legal and regulatory laws in our city. It is probably the first thing you should check out when you consider hosting on Airbnb®.

PLEASE CHECK OUT YOUR LOCAL LAWS BEFORE LISTING YOUR SPACE!

Some cities have become very annoyed that Airbnb® has taken off like a racehorse at the track, and they're not getting a piece of the occupancy tax that so many cities tack onto that hotel bill.

Make sure you can legally operate a B & B in your area.

Likewise, if you rent or lease your apartment or home, it is extremely important that you have permission from your landlord to operate a B & B.

The city in which I live allows Airbnb®, and I own my home, so those two were a "thumbs up" and we were good to go!

We set out to create a comfortable, clean, and well-appointed guest rental: one that would ensure privacy and a great experience. We wanted our guests to step into the space and feel welcome, with all the amenities included; from tasteful décor to small details like a luggage rack, robes, and a bottle of wine.

Having a self-contained apartment made it easy to consider all kinds of guest combinations. We have had couples, families, business people, singles and even a few babies. Our other home has 4 bedrooms; we rent out 2 of them during special times of the year. We stay in the master bedroom; the two other rooms are on the other side of the house and share a bathroom. We take adults only for that rental as the rooms are very close together and a crying baby will be heard through the walls.

Another question is: how often do you want guests in your home?

It is very easy to block off the calendar and put your rooms up only for weekend or holiday rental time. I have a friend whose children see their father every other weekend. She rents out the master bedroom and stays in the kids' room when they are off with Daddy.

How many guests in the room is one more consideration, as well as coordinating sharing the kitchen and bathroom. I have one friend who only takes women guests, and some other friends who prefer men guests. It's all about what you are comfortable doing, and remember, you get to choose who stays with you!

So to recap, these are the important questions to ask yourself:

- ✓ **Is it legal and permitted to have an Airbnb® in my home, apartment, castle, etc.?**

- ✓ **Which room(s) do I want to rent out?**

- ✓ **How many people per room?**

- ✓ **Who am I comfortable renting to?**

- ✓ **How often do I want to rent out my space?**

If the answers to these questions fall in the positive direction, let's get started!

Chapter 2 - How Airbnb® works

Once you have made the decision to become a host with Airbnb®, the first thing to do is to sign up on their website. This takes some time as there are verifications, photos to be uploaded, and financial information to be entered. They run a background check on every prospective host to the best of their ability, and check out your social media (FaceBook and LinkedIn) profiles to match up information. There is also a telephone and email match and an interface with your financial institution. You will give them your taxpayer identification, as you are sent a Form 1099 (in the USA) to use for your taxes.

Being a host is a responsibility, and making someone feel special is HUGE! As stated earlier, the host is the brand. Think about it. Do you remember the desk clerk who checked you in at that name brand hotel? No? How about the Airbnb® host who left you homemade gluten free vegan cookies and fresh flowers? Yes? Okay!

Soon after your listing is "LIVE" you will start to get inquiries from prospective guests. The Airbnb® mobile app is extremely valuable to have when you are away from a computer, and you can also elect to get booking requests via text message. I choose both as I do not want to miss a prospective booking.

Answer the inquiry as soon as possible, and give them a chance to tell you a little about themselves and check out their verifications. Many first time users have incomplete profiles, so I urge them to complete the process and offer help if needed.

Once their guest profile is completed, feel free to ask them questions. If you like the answers, go ahead and pre-approve them. I also send them a message urging them to book, and wish them a wonderful day!

Your payout comes after the guest checks out, or during their stay if they have a long visit. I have had a few prospective guests ask if they can circumvent paying on Airbnb®'s website and pay us directly. Our answer is a resounding "NO". If they insist or ask again, we decline their request.

After the guest departs, both you and the guest will receive a request to review each other. After both sides submit the reviews, they are visible for both to see. Reviews go into a rating algorithm, along with response time and a few other magical ingredients, and are then cooked up to get your host rating. It can also win you the SuperHost award, like we did in 2014 and 2015!

Along the way, if you have any questions or concerns, Airbnb® has a fantastic host support area with live people to talk to, an extensive frequently asked question section, and a very speedy email response.

Your neighborhood has a major impact on your listing. Just like the old saying in real estate: Location, Location, Location. There are two main ways in which the neighborhood impacts your rental. First, each neighborhood has a unique day of the week demand curve based on the type of travelers that visit your neighborhood. Secondly, travelers access your listing in comparison to nearby/similar listings. Therefore, the price you can charge for your home must be partially determined by how well your listing performs in comparison to nearby listings. Airbnb® travelers often search for listings based on neighborhood, price, and number of rooms.

So to recap:

- ✓ **Sign up on the Airbnb® website (www.airbnb.com)**
- ✓ **Download mobile app**
- ✓ **Answer inquiries as soon as possible, and urge them to book with you**
- ✓ **Payout is through the website, no cash changes hands**
- ✓ **Review your guest immediately**
- ✓ **Contact Airbnb® by email or phone with any questions or concerns**

Chapter 3 - Listing Your Space

Basically a beautifully and well-done listing is your entree to making money. It is this advertisement of you and your space that should reflect your best efforts in marketing. Be honest and make sure that your listing accurately reflects what your guest can experience. It is also important to be good to yourself and set up a basic framework of guest rules.

Remember it is your house, and you get to decide who stays there and rules you wish to have followed. The next few steps are the key elements to getting bookings!

1. **Fill out your Airbnb® profile and include a recent HAPPY** photo with as much detail as you can possibly fit into the box. You are a real person and not a model or actor depicted on a hotel ad or website. The listing must be used solely for lodging.

2. **Clear and honest communications are key**. Let the potential guests know what you have available, and what may be obtainable nearby. The more accurate and true to your listing, the better the reviews. As Airbnb® is international, what may be the norm in the US or Canada may differ in Europe or Asia. If

listing a mobile home, yacht, or other vessel, it must be permanently attached to its set location for the length of the booking. If a listing doesn't meet the Airbnb® guidelines, they may exercise their discretion to limit, suspend or deactivate it, or even cancel the host's account. If in doubt about your listing's qualifications, please review Airbnb®'s Terms of Service on the website.

3. **Book the Airbnb® photographer to shoot the photos of your space.** It is a free service, and your photos will be stamped "Airbnb® Verified". It is another layer of reassurance to the guest that what they see is what they get. The photographers are experienced in making "good" look "great" and carry an assortment of wide angle lenses to capture even the tiniest of bedrooms.

Remember: A picture is worth a thousand words, or maybe even a thousand bookings!

You are now an entrepreneur, find your right price. We looked at comparable spaces in the area to get an idea what others were charging. Go to your neighborhood, filter the number of bedrooms, similar spaces and click on the calendar and see how booked up they are. We tweaked our prices until we found our sweet spot and added a modest cleaning fee. It is the same amount we pay our cleaning crew. If you are booking up too quickly, chances are your price is too low. If occupancy is your goal, then a low price will insure that! Do you want more guests and less money or more money and fewer guests? More than 50% of guests book 30 days or less in advance. If you are booked months in advance, please review your pricing! A security deposit is also optional.

In the beginning, we decided not to include a security deposit. Unfortunately, some guests broke our rules and smoked in our apartment for four days. We had to ask them to leave before their two week stay was over and hire a heavy cleaning crew. The place had to be aired for three days, and we lost out on 11 days of revenue. Of course, if there is no damage, the security deposit will be refunded!

Some hosts charge more for weekends and holiday periods, a discount for week or longer stays, low traffic times, or special prices for events such as festivals or sports tournaments. Again it will depend on your market, so work with it until you find your winning combo. Service fees of 3% of what you charge your guest will be automatically subtracted by Airbnb® before you receive your payout. They also charge the guest fees on a sliding scale of 6-12 % on top of your charges. Another idea is using the suggestions from Airbnb® and their new pricing guidelines. This is an interesting situation for the host and the guest, as Airbnb® must walk the line for both parties. Their pricing is not automatic, and you must go on the site daily and accept the new prices. There are a number of Third Party Service Providers who will do Dynamic Pricing for you. Companies such as BeyondPricing.com use an algorithm to change the prices daily based on supply and demand.

4. **As demand changes, so do prices.** There are three factors in determining dynamic pricing: Seasonality, Day of Week, and Events. Seasonality differs in every city, as does day of week. For example some urban centers may be heavy on the business traveler during the week, where a beach resort may be hot in the summer and cold in the winter. Event impact, such as the Super Bowl or Rose Parade is a highly localized factor. It is up to you to make the final pricing decisions.

5. **Communicate with everyone who makes an inquiry.** Some people are new to the site and unsure how it works.

Gently lead them by the hand and respond sooner rather than later. Even if your place is booked, your kindness and helpfulness may be remembered for a booking at a later date. It has happened to us a few times! **Remind them the early bird gets the room!**

6. **Be yourself and share your neighborhood**! Most guests want to blend into the local scene and appreciate you just being yourself. Tell them about special events in the area like festivals, little known nature walks, and hole in the wall taco stands. If they had wanted bland, boring and corporate, they wouldn't have chosen to stay with you!

7. **Pets and Kids may not be congruent with your living situation.** Many folks are allergic to animal hair and a crying infant may not be a welcome addition in the next room. Make sure you state who you are comfortable having on your property. We have two short haired dogs and they are acknowledged in our profile. We make parents aware there are stairs in the apartment, so please bring appropriate child safety gates, portable playpens and other infant supplies as

needed. It is up to you if you wish to charge an extra person fee for children. For us, up to two years old get a free stay, over two is an extra fee.

8. **Listing multiple rooms within the house is very easy.** Have the photographer takes photos of the entire house and then create a separate listing for each room. You can use the same photos of the exterior of the home, kitchen, and bathroom and then add your specific bedroom. You can also cut and paste the general descriptions and other info pertaining to the house. Price each of them separately and they will be listed under your account. Guests must book each room separately, and if they want multiple rooms or the entire house, you can make them a Special Offer. It is a little tricky the first time, but after that it becomes very easy. The hardest part was syncing the calendar to reflect availability. We have a home in Palm Desert, CA where we rent out separate rooms only during specific times of the year. It was very fun to have so many combinations of guests for three weekends in a row! Although there are three rooms available, we decided after two were filled we

would block off the third room and keep it available in case friends or family showed up at the last minute. Relatives from Australia ended up passing through and added a lot of laughter and hilarity to the weekend's activities.

9. **Make it easy on yourself**. Track all your expenses for your Airbnb®. Set up a separate bank account exclusively for your new business with credit and debit cards. Keep all your receipts for future tax deductions. Meet with your financial professional and plan for the taxes associated with your new income.

After you have filled in every nook and cranny on the Airbnb® host listing page— hit the List button and your listing will go public in about 12 hours!

Get ready!!!

Chapter 4 - Setting up your space

The first thoughts that came to mind when I imagined having guests at my home was to spoil them with special treats and luxuries. I have stayed at quite a few five star hotel properties throughout my travels, and loved the beautiful gifts and surprises left in my room. I decided to go the extra step and really put a lot of thought into thinking about everything I would want when staying at someone's home. When, I travel and stay in hotels, I usually have to call housekeeping for more towels, a robe, extra pillow, etc. Giving the guests the feeling they were staying with special friends in a small cozy home with luxurious treats and surprises was the intention.

So, depending on your space(s) you have in mind, the first suggestion I have is:

Clear out the clutter and clean your home top to bottom! Have friends come by and give it the white glove test. Putting your personal mark on the décor is one way to create a unique space, however limit the personal items. A photo of you and your prom date in 1976 may be cool for you but not real decorative for the guests.

Once you have cleared and cleaned, take an inventory of the towels, sheets, pillows and bed linens you plan to use. It is advisable to have non-allergenic type pillows, as feathers and down bother many people. Anything looking worn out, faded, stained, and tattered should be put in the pile for donation to charity.

Depending on guest traffic, it is advisable to have a few sets of sheets and towels ready in case of accidents or spills. It always amazes me how a single guy could go through 8 towels in 2 nights, whereas a family of three only used 4 towels in 5 days! I guess his motto was "It was there, so I used it!"

We wanted the bedroom to be restful and simple so we used clean lines of soothing color. We added a colorful lithograph of the local coastline, a homemade candle on the bed table and comfortable, non-allergenic bedding.

Shopping Tip: We found the bedding at IKEA to be of fine quality and great value. It's simple, bright, and we have three sets of interchangeable bed linens.

Guests get their own shelves in the fridge and pantry The majority of our guests are extremely happy when they see the well-stocked kitchen. Although most of them do not prepare seven course meals, there have been some pretty great meals cooked there! We had a traveling farm to table chef stay with us for four days and he prepped and cooked a lot of the dishes that turned up on someone's table! Lucky them!

When guests stay inside our Palm Desert house, they are given their own shelves in the fridge, as well as space in the pantry if needed. We provide them with coffee and teas and breakfast items every morning, and they are welcome to use spices, oils, or about anything-all they need to do is ask!

Bathroom schedules are extremely important if guests are staying inside the home and sharing a bathroom with you. Coordinating the schedule so everyone can be accommodated is a great idea. Ask them when they need it in the morning, and let them know what time you get ready for work. Again, keeping it clean and tidy is important, as is changing out the towels and keeping everything stocked like toilet tissue, soap and shampoo.

Other Must-Haves include:

- ☐ Unexpected treats and surprises like a jar of candy, flower bouquet, bottle of wine
- ☐ Wi-Fi access information with password typed on a card
- ☐ Parking locations and rules (free beats fees at a hotel garage!)
- ☐ Guidebook with information about the local area, brochures, shopping, day trips, and sightseeing activities.
- ☐ Ironing board and Iron
- ☐ Emergency card with host's cell number and local hospital information

Chapter 5 - Communication

You just received a notification from the Airbnb® mobile app, (**LOVE** that sound it makes!) and you have a communication from a prospective guest! **The two basic types of communications you will receive are booking inquiries and request for a reservation.**

A booking inquiry is in the form of a question such as: Is the space available from this date to that date? We have a baby traveling with us, do you have a portable crib? How far is Disneyland? Do you live in a safe neighborhood? Believe it or not, those are real questions I have received! Some are fishing around and some are serious. I treat all inquiries as if they're serious.

A request for a reservation is just that—they want to book your place, right now! I take a look at their account profile, then ask a few questions: Who will they be traveling with? What is their intention for visiting my city? Do they need any help with attractions and plans while they will be visiting? What time do they expect to arrive? Based upon the answers, I will usually pre-approve them and then tell them to please go ahead and book their stay.

Responding quickly to both types of communications is of utmost importance.

Airbnb® measures host responsiveness and it plays a part in how your listing comes up in searches. They use a host response rate tracker and it is a key factor in the search rankings. Airbnb® give you 24 hours to respond, and it is counted down on the message threads.

RESPOND TO EVERY INQUIRY AND REQUEST, IF ONLY TO SAY IT IS NOT AVAILABLE AT THIS TIME! Although it may be unavailable for that time slot, you can ask them to please reconsider your place next time!

Once they have booked, you will be given their contact information in the form of their phone number and a special email created for them by Airbnb®. They will get your exact address and your phone number as well. None of the hosts' personal information beyond their first name is given on the listing page. It is very important to keep in touch with the guests prior to arrival, and I usually text or email them about two or three days in advance of their arrival.

We like to personally welcome each guest, explain the house rules, make sure they are comfortable with their accommodations and answer any questions about the local area. Once they check in, they are given a card with contact information to carry with them in case of emergency. Sometimes because of flight schedules or long distance driving, they arrive late, so I make sure there is a key available and clear parking instructions. I will check in with them the next day.

It is important to takes cues from the guest and gauge how much attention they require from you. Some guests are chatty and full of questions, while some are content to get the key, Wi-Fi password and call it a night. Guests experience occasional challenges, and again having the emergency information card is important. We had a young couple stay with us who were involved in a bad traffic accident. They were taken to a faraway hospital and their car was totaled. Luckily, they had put our card in their wallet and we were called to pick them up upon their discharge from the hospital. We went into to full Mother-mode and stopped by the drugstore to get them their prescriptions, chicken soup, and cold packs to put on their bruises. They were bed-bound the rest of their stay, but we took care of them until a family member was able to get them back to the east coast. We have had power blackouts, earthquakes, toilets stopped up, and the worst thing possible—running out of toilet tissue!

It is interesting to note that the guests who experienced problems that were gracefully resolved, ended up giving the best reviews! One couple stayed the weekend to attend a wedding, and the bridesmaid's dress never showed up! She was about the same size as my daughter, so I offered to loan her a dress to wear. Although she didn't borrow the dress, she did write a glowing review of our generosity.

It has been, and will continue to be, our intention to treat our guests as we wish to be treated, not merely as a business transaction.

One of the benefits of using Airbnb® is that no money changes hands. All the financials are done on the website. Beware of inquiries trying to make a side deal off-line. Airbnb®'s communications block phone numbers and email addresses. We have had some pleas asking stay here for free (really?), others wanting to stay for a hugely reduced rate (that is negotiable, feel free to state your price and stick with it). It has been our experience those kinds of situations are time wasters and so if it smells like a duck, it is a DUCK!

One of the many benefits of hosting on Airbnb® is getting to know people from all over the world and making new friends. One woman and her husband came to stay with us for ten days to visit relatives nearby. We realized we had several mutual friends, and they have come back to stay with us multiple times. Another woman from China came with her daughter, a recent Ivy League graduate. The daughter was job hunting, and we were happy to set her up with an executive recruiter friend who landed her some interviews.

Reviews are important!

Whether a compliment or helpful feedback, we turn in guest reviews as soon as possible after departure. We stay positive in our approach, knowing everyone has unique challenges. However, getting a guest review stating they ran out of toilet tissue because their toddler threw it in the bathtub is a bit ridiculous! All they needed to do was ask for more, and it would have been sent right up! According to Airbnb® statistics, guests are more likely to review their host after their host reviews them! We want everyone to have their best experience possible, so we encourage our guests to communicate with us as soon as possible.

Our checkout time is 12 Noon, and we have a two hour window to clean and prepare for the next guests. So far, we have experienced one challenge in "encouraging" our guests to say good-bye. We had a cleaning crew standing by, and the young lady and her boyfriend were having quite a heated "something". Fortunately, the next guests had dropped their bags off earlier and gone to the beach! Our cleaning crew made several forceful knocks on the door and the guests finally left. Since that incident, it has been smooth sailing, but always be prepared to summon your inner warrior!

Chapter 6 - Reservations

In the previous chapter we learned there are two types of communications you will receive:

1. Booking inquiry with questions for the host from a prospective guest.
2. Booking request to make reservations.

Remember—You are the decision maker as to whom you want in your home!

Carefully read their profile, look at their photo, read reviews from other hosts. Be honest and open with any questions they may have of you, and ask them questions too! If someone has a bare bones profile with no photo, ask them if they are new to Airbnb®, and suggest they put in more information so you can make a more informed decision on their booking. It is important to be satisfied with the answers to your questions, and if in doubt you can decline their reservation request. Consider if you wish to use the Instant Book feature. That gives guests the power to book without making an inquiry first. Many people want to get a room and be done with that aspect of their trip, and will look for Instant Book when choosing on Airbnb®. I recently planned a trip to Paris, and it was very frustrating for me waiting to hear back from hosts on an inquiry. Some never answered me at all! The flip side on Instant Book is you have to accept the booking, no matter who it is. That doesn't work for me, as we get many inquiries to film on the property.

With Instant Book there would be a mini film studio in progress much of the time!

Begin by taking one night bookings

You are in charge of setting the price per night, as well as the minimum nights for a booking.

We started with a minimum of one night for our reservations in order to build up our reviews. A guest who stays one night carries the same weight in the review ratings as someone who stays multiple nights.

So, although it may seem awkward at first, start out taking one night reservations.

As many hosts do not do this, you may get many bookings because you are the only one in the area who does! Once you have several good reviews under your belt, you can choose to change the minimum number of nights, as well as weekend and holiday requirements.

Once you have accepted the request for booking hit the Pre-Approve button!

Hitting the Pre-Approval button will send them a message that you want them to commit to the dates they have asked for. I usually send them a message telling them they are Pre-Approved, and urging them to book.

Have a Calendar dedicated to Airbnb® Bookings

Once the reservation is confirmed, I take the Guest's name and contact information and write it on a special calendar for Airbnb® bookings.

I color code the guest's name and write in their estimated time of arrival.

While this information is stored on your listing profile and on the mobile app, I find it easier to keep track of guests, maintenance workers, and housekeeping when written out and color coded.

EXAMPLE OF BOOKING CALENDAR

MARCH 2015

Sunday	Monday	Tuesday	Wednesday	Thursday	Friday	Saturday
1	2	3	4 *Leslie & Chris from Hilo 245-6411*	5	6	7 *Susie B-day*
8	9 *Mike S.*	10	11	12	13	14
15 *John & Kathy King (will ch in late)*	16	17	18	19	20	21 *McKenny's (anniversary)*
22	23	24 *Ron & Beth 989-3277*	25	26	27 *PLUMBERS*	28
29 *Jeanne 345-6400*	30	31	Notes			

Even though there are lots of computerized calendar systems, I've found that a paper calendar with lines works best.

I use color coded markers for different things like confirmed reservations, blocked out for personal friends and family stays, cleaning and maintenance days, and other related activities.

It also allows me to write in names, contact numbers, and any special notes concerning the booking itself.

Because it's paper, I can move it from place to place and have it with me when I'm on the phone – even my mobile phone.

You can Google *"Calendar Templates"* and find hundreds of different styles that you can download and print for free.

Cancellations

The guests are counting on you now, so canceling them can be extremely disruptive. Airbnb® recognizes there are extenuating circumstances, and it is important to discuss with them your reason for canceling the guests. Be aware, you may face cancellation penalties.

We have had two cancellation requests from guests. One woman realized she had scheduled an "important" dental appointment in Boston the same day she had booked our apartment. Since, we live near Los Angeles, we thought something was a little fishy about this booking. We called Airbnb®, explained the situation and decided to go ahead and cancel her. Apparently, we saved her from paying us the two nights she booked, which someone else ended up taking. We chalked it off to a learning experience, and also made sure to set our cancellation policy to strict. It is up to you to establish your cancellation policy, so carefully review the descriptions on the website when making your setting.

The other cancellation request was made by a guy who was coming to meet up with his girlfriend in LA, then driving to our home in Palm Desert to attend a music festival. They broke up after he made the booking, and she kept the tickets to the festival. He was going to get 50% of the reservation cost refunded and he wanted us to cancel him so he would get 100% back. I reminded him of our "Strict Cancellation" policy and denied his request. Apparently, he went to Airbnb® and presented them with a doctor's note stating he was unable to travel due to medical limitations, and Airbnb® elected to refund him in full. The good news is someone else quickly booked the room once it was canceled in the system!

It is important to keep in mind that stuff happens and be willing to go with the flow! I know another host whose roof top pool leaked into her ceiling and turned her apartment into a swamp. Her guest was into week two of a five week booking. The host made arrangements with a friend to put the guest up temporarily in her home for free; then they contacted Airbnb® and found her other lodgings.

Altering reservations

Sometimes plans change and it is very easy to alter dates. Extending or reducing dates of stay is a breeze. Simply go to the reservation page, find the guest and click on "alter reservation". A drop down with dates will come up and simply change the dates. In a situation with multiple rooms, it is quite simple to switch rooms as well. The guest will receive a request to alter the reservation, they click approve, and it is done.

When Guests Break the Rules

We had two young European men check in with us for a two week stay. They said they were here for a movie deal and excited to be in LA for their first time. Upon check in, they noticed the No Smoking sign in the apartment as well as No Smoking listed in our house rules. They asked if they could smoke outside, and I told them yes. I put a receptacle outdoors for their ashes and butts.

Two nights later, my sister and I had friends over who wanted to see the guest quarters. We knocked on the door and smoke came billowing out. Every room was consumed with the acrid smell of heavy smoking. Needless to say, my blood was boiling as we told them "It smells like smoke in here." One of them turned crimson as the other said "We smoked outside on the balcony and it came through the door." After they departed for their night's activities, my sister and her friend (also an AirBnB Host) told me they needed to go. Her friend's experience with guests who broke agreements, said they were apt to keep breaking them during their stay. I was relieved we caught them smoking only three nights into their stay, as it would have been a major disaster after 14 nights of smoking damage.

As a result of this incident, we have decided there will be no smoking or "vaping" on our property. We also decided to add a nominal security deposit to all bookings going forward, even though the Host Guarantee program promises to help pay for damages. (Guests will receive a refund if there is no damage to my apartment!)

I phoned AirBnB Host support and was given three options:

Option #1 - Cancel their stay and tell them to pack their bags and get out. This option was not utilized since it contained a possible Host Penalty. Even though they damaged my property and violated the guest agreement, a cancellation could be a negative in my Host profile and ratings.

Option #2 - Let them stay the whole 14 nights, believe they were not smoking, and be saddled with a massive smoke clean up problem after they left. Not an option for me!

Option #3 - Alter their reservation so they would be departing after 5 nights instead of 14 nights, and add a heavy duty cleaning fee. Refund the difference of the total they had already paid, minus the nights stayed and cleaning fees.

This was the most appealing. After communicating through the Airbnb® message center, I sent them the following message:

Dear X:

When you checked in on Thursday night, you asked me about smoking. I told you that you can smoke on the patio and put an ashtray out for you. There are no smoking signs in the apartment, in the rules, and in the agreement to stay at my home. When we went inside on Saturday night, we smelled smoke in every room. This causes damage to my property and is a serious violation of our agreement.

I am sending you an alteration to check out on Monday and return the key and gate opener to me by 12 noon in person. I am also asking for an extra fee to have a deep cleaning for the smoke damage.

Please understand this is my business and I expected you to follow the contract as you agreed to respect my rules.

Thank you in advance,

Roxanne

They agreed to the alteration and ended up leaving Sunday night, instead of Monday noon. I cleaned and aired out the place for 3 days and was able to get the smell out.

When in doubt, call the Host Resolution center. They have a toll free number, open 24 hours, 7 days a week!

Stay up to date with messages on your Airbnb® Host Home section

It is important to keep up with the communications you will receive through the message box. Sometimes it may be a question, other times a request to extend a stay, or just about anything.

You can set it up so communications come through as text messages, email, and on the mobile app. I chose it to come through all 3 for maximum visibility and responsiveness.

Non-traditional guest reservations

Airbnb® is being used increasing by business travelers and commercial enterprises. What appears to be a standard inquiry at first, may later be revealed to be a producer looking for a filming location, or a logistics manager seeking lodging for employees while on the road.

We received requests to use our apartment for a TV reality show, two student films, and a commercial. Again, it is up to you to decide who or what you want going on in your space. My sister and I have both had experience in the entertainment world and know legitimate productions carry insurance and have a budget for location shoots. We also know there is a lot of equipment, noise, cars and people to deal with on even a small shoot. So in considering all those factors, we declined the requests thus far to use our apartment for filming.

Another interesting reservation request came from the transportation manager of a "Farm to Table" catering company. She wanted to book the space for herself and a visiting chef and asked if they could park their bus in our driveway! My radar went up when I heard "bus", but I let her know there was ample street parking around the corner. Both parties were coming on separate flights, and checking in late, so I left the key out for them.

The next morning three people exited the apartment. As the woman who booked had a photo on her Airbnb® account showing her with light hair and eyes, it was evident none of the three fit the bill! I asked them their names and was told "Jane" went to Vermont for a funeral. My gut feeling was that I was being played, so I called Airbnb® customer service for hosts. I was given the opportunity to evict the three of them, let them stay and add an "extra person fee", or let it play out.

As I mulled over the situation, I received a call from "Jane" in Vermont. It seemed she had dropped her phone at the airport and it shattered. She retrieved my number from the Airbnb® website and apologized for her co-workers not following instructions. She also told me she wasn't coming after all, and made an impassioned request to let one of the three, the chef, stay, as he had flown in from Iowa to do the job. I made the decision to let him stay, and she also booked him an extra night. He turned out to be a really nice person, and the only negative from the experience was since "Jane" booked the apartment but didn't personally stay, no review was left.

Chapter 7 - Long Term Guests

Having long term guests is an interesting situation. Tenancy laws differ widely in the United States, **so if you wish to have someone in your space over 30 days, please check your local laws.** In Illinois, New York, and California a residential tenancy may be created after 30 consecutive nights. We bypassed this by putting our maximum nights' stay at 28 nights.

We received a request from a visiting nurse to stay at our place for 13 weeks. She was on a contract to a nearby hospital and really liked our listing. She also requested a special price, and after a few messages and emails, we arrived on a price that suited both parties. She booked the apartment for 28 days on the Airbnb® website. That gave us both a trial period to see if she liked it and we liked her. Also, the period she booked was an extremely slow time of year and we were going to be traveling much of the time. Not having to worry about having multiple guests come and go was a bit of a relief. Luckily, it was a good match for both sides, and with the help of a realtor, we wrote up a tenancy agreement to allow her to stay on after 28 days. Again, **contact a landlord-tenant expert in your area who is extremely versed in your local laws.**

According to the Airbnb® website, guests who refuse to leave are a rare situation. There is an Airbnb® 24/7 support team available to work with you to resolve the problem. It is a good idea to know your rights as they may affect your ability to evict a guest who overstays their reservation, so please contact a landlord-tenant expert in your area before considering long-term bookings.

Chapter 8 - Emergencies

Being a host has inherent responsibilities that we have taken very seriously in certain situations. By far the worst emergency situation we have so far encountered was when our guests were involved in a traffic accident, and ended up in the emergency ward. Their car was totaled and towed away from the accident scene, the woman's purse was in the car with her glasses and ID, and she and her friend ended up at County General on a Saturday night. In other words, nightmare come true on a vacation! Luckily, her friend had our card we give to all our guests and the hospital was able to call us upon their discharge. We scooped them up, brought them back here, and nursed them until a relative was able to pick them up.

Another host I know had a long-term guest staying in her penthouse apartment. Her place was in Los Angeles and she had left for a week to attend a conference in New York. The second day she was in New York, the ceiling caved in as it was soaked with water from the leaking swimming pool on the roof. The guest called the host screaming in fear, and the host contacted a friend to get her out of the apartment! The guest was put up for a night at the friend's house, and Airbnb® found her other lodgings the next day. The apartment was condemned and the host had to retrieve her soaked and ruined items and move on as well.

It is important to be prepared for emergencies that occur in your specific region, and in Los Angeles, that means earthquakes. We have only experienced one minor quake since our Airbnb® opened. The guests were at an amusement park, so didn't notice anything. It is a good idea to have some supplies conveniently located in your space for guests just in case something BIG occurs.

Another consideration is purchasing home sharing liability insurance. There are several companies offering this type of insurance, and a good website to check out is Peers.org. Airbnb® is the only company as of this writing that includes liability insurance for hosts, but their coverage applies only to home sharing through the Airbnb® site. If you are registering your space with multiple home sharing websites, it is a good idea to have your insurance professional review your homeowner's/renter's coverages. I am not an insurance agent, so I consult with the experts when in doubt!

In the case of natural disasters, such as hurricanes, earthquakes, and tornadoes, Airbnb® has a disaster response platform where hosts can offer lodging for a discount or even free. If it is free, Airbnb® waives all service fees. When disaster strikes, Airbnb® activates their response tool for the affected area. Hosts receive an email asking if they are able to help. Existing hosts and local residents with the extra space can host those in need for free.

Finally, Airbnb® offered a free "Home Safety Kit for Hosts" on the website. The price was right, so I ordered it. The kit is actually a card with two magnets on the back to put on the refrigerator! It has spaces to fill in the emergency phone number (911 in the U.S.), nearest hospital or medical center, first aid kit location, fire extinguisher location, and emergency exit instructions.

Chapter 9 - Checklists and Helpful Tips

This guide was written with a quick and easy checklist method for each room your guest will use. The first checklist will be for set-up, stocking, and replenishing; the second checklist will be for the cleaning crew (even if it is you!).

By printing out each of the checklists, you will ensure all bases are covered for your next guest's stay. Some hosts also have an inventory list they refer to when the guest checks out. You can do that one on your own with video, photos, or a checklist. To our knowledge, nothing has been taken from our unit.

In most of our 5 star reviews, cleanliness is mentioned on each and every one! It is absolutely imperative to have a spotlessly clean, tidy, and good smelling place for your guests to stay.

We request our guests text our cleaning crew upon checkout. We quickly change all linens, wash towels, and replenish food supplies as soon as possible. After the cleaning crew finishes, we go over the checklist again. Sometimes, we have only 2 hours to get our apartment back in check-in perfect condition.

The Bathroom Stocking Checklist:

Many of these items can be the mini bottles you get at hotels, or use refillable glass canisters to limit the amount of plastic that needs to be recycled!

Shopping Tip: *The 99cents store and Target are great for bathroom items.*

- ☐ Shower Gel (leaves no soap scum)
- ☐ Body lotion
- ☐ Comfy bath mats (2 sets)
- ☐ Cotton swabs and cotton squares
- ☐ Shower cap
- ☐ Shampoo and Conditioner
- ☐ Towels—8 each: Bath size, hand towels, wash cloths
- ☐ Extra toilet and facial tissue
- ☐ Liquid hand soap (leaves no soap scum)
- ☐ Toothbrush and floss
- ☐ First Aid kit
- ☐ Clean shower curtains

<u>Optional—But Highly Recommended:</u>

- ☐ Magnifying mirror
- ☐ Air freshener/diffuser
- ☐ Terry cloth robes (2)

Bathroom Cleaning Checklist:

- ☐ Toilet
- ☐ Bath tub/shower/shower curtain
- ☐ Sink and countertop
- ☐ Mirrors (including magnifying mirror)
- ☐ Fresh towels and bathmat
- ☐ Clear out and clean drawers
- ☐ Replenish: shower gel, shampoo, conditioner, hand soap
- ☐ Refill: Cotton swabs and cotton pads
- ☐ Empty trash and replace bag
- ☐ Mop floor

Bedroom Stocking Checklist:

Shopping tip: *We found the bedding at IKEA to be of fine quality and great value! Keep it simple and clean.*

- ☐ Mattress pads—2: waterproof, one on bed, and one clean and ready
- ☐ Sheets—3 sets: one on bed, and two clean and ready
- ☐ Comforters: 2 of the same, interchangeable with pillow shams and sheets. One on the bed and one clean and ready to go.
- ☐ Blankets—2: one for winter and one for summer (depending on your climate)
- ☐ Pillows—4: non-allergenic
- ☐ Rugs—2: one on the floor, other clean and ready
- ☐ Bed tables with reading lamps
- ☐ Box of matching facial tissues
- ☐ Optional: Candle/potpourri

<u>Bedroom Cleaning Checklist:</u>

- ☐ Change out all bed linens including: comforter, pillow shams and mattress pad
- ☐ Dust bed tables and dressers
- ☐ Check drawers and under the bed!
- ☐ Dust window sills and blinds
- ☐ Vacuum

<u>Kitchen Stocking Checklist:</u>

(This checklist was written for an apartment that is used exclusively for Airbnb® guests. If your guests are staying inside your home, this list will most likely include everything you already have in your kitchen.)

- ☐ Coffee machine (such as a Keurig or Mr. Coffee) that also makes hot water to use in teas, instant hot chocolate and instant oatmeal.
- ☐ Mugs, glasses, plates, bowls, forks, knives and spoons
- ☐ Knife block with knives
- ☐ Pots and pans
- ☐ Cookie sheets
- ☐ Cooking utensils
- ☐ Wine opener
- ☐ Can opener
- ☐ Oven mitts, dish towels, potholders
- ☐ Dish rack, pot scrubbers, sponges

Optional and highly recommended:

☐ Blender

☐ French press coffee pot

☐ Hospitality station with: coffee pods, tea bags, creamers, nuts, snack mix, microwave popcorn, instant oatmeal

☐ Unexpected treats and surprises like a jar of candies, fresh bouquet, or freshly made cookies!!!

☐ In the refrigerator: water bottles, sodas, juice, bottle of wine, jar of miniature chocolates or candies

☐ In the pantry: spices, cooking oils and tin foil, shopping bags

☐ Fire extinguisher

☐ Portable heater and fan

☐ Extra blankets

☐ Earthquake kit

<u>Kitchen Cleaning Checklist:</u>

- ☐ Clean stove, oven, and microwave
- ☐ Wash and put away dishes
- ☐ Wipe window sill and blinds
- ☐ Clean counters and scrub sink
- ☐ Refill dish soap dispenser
- ☐ Paper and cloth towels
- ☐ Replace sponge
- ☐ Restock Refrigerator
- ☐ 2x waters
- ☐ 2x sodas/juices
- ☐ Bottle of wine
- ☐ Fill up chocolates or other goodies
- ☐ Replenish the optional (but highly recommended), snack tray:
- ☐ 4x coffee pods
- ☐ Assorted tea bags
- ☐ Individual creamers
- ☐ 2x bags of trail mix
- ☐ 2x breakfast bars
- ☐ 2x instant hot chocolate
- ☐ Remove all trash
- ☐ Mop kitchen floor

<u>Living Room Cleaning Checklist:</u>

- ☐ Change sofa cover
- ☐ Check underneath cushions and bottom of sofa for trash and other items
- ☐ Fluff pillows
- ☐ Wipe down TV remote controls
- ☐ Arrange brochures and welcome area
- ☐ Dust window sills
- ☐ Vacuum/mop floor

House Rules:

Dear Guests:

In order to make your stay an enjoyable one, we ask that you please observe the following rules:

- ✓ Please remove shoes upon entering
- ✓ No additional occupants other than at the time of booking
- ✓ No smoking, vaping or e-cigarettes on the property
- ✓ No illegal or unlawful activities
- ✓ No parties or guests
- ✓ No pets
- ✓ Please empty trash upon your departure
- ✓ In order to keep costs down, and so guests can benefit, please do not take items from the unit

We wish you a beautiful stay, and thank you for honoring these agreements.

Thank you in advance!

Peace and Blessings,
The Lawrence Family

Confirmed Guest Checklist:

- ☐ As soon as booking is confirmed, you will receive a reservation number.

- ☐ Enter the guest's name and contact information on your booking calendar and color code them.

- ☐ Email or text 2 days before arrival to get their ETA.

- ☐ Offer to answer any questions and let them know you are grateful they chose to stay with you!

- ☐ Greet them personally at check-in time. If not possible, leave the key in a pre-arranged secure spot.

- ☐ Give a tour of the premises; explain House Rules, emergency contact information, WI-FI, and check out times and procedures.

Chapter 10 - Third Party Service Providers

As of this writing, there are all kinds of startups happening around Airbnb® and other home sharing services. Springing up like apps on an iPhone, these services mostly came out of the desires of hosts who want to make things better for their guests and easier for themselves. Some address the most common problems seen and help to deal with entry (picking up and dropping off keys), pricing, safety, and a high standard of cleanliness. Some of the companies are in selected markets in the US, while others are worldwide.

Many hosts find that automating time consuming tasks give them more time to focus on marketing and booking rates. Here are some of the companies you may wish to explore once you have your place up and running: *(Note the information below is from the services' websites)*

- www.Guesty.com: Guesty handles all guest communication, schedules cleanings, and coordinates key exchange. Optimizes price for more bookings. Charge: 3% of each booking with a minimum of $3 per booking. Manages only Airbnb®, operates in selected cities in the US.

- www.Keycafe.com: Keycafe is an easy way to manage access to your home online without any upfront costs or hardware installation. Locations in NYC, San Francisco, Seattle and soon Austin. Charge: $7.95/month plus $1.95 per key pick up.

- www.ALL-SET.com Hands on management of keys, cleaning, and concierge support in the Chicago area.

- www.hurdlr.com Offers Host Finance Management

- www.CityCopilot.com: Key exchange for guests, luggage storage, package acceptance. Host turnover packages include cleaning, fresh linens, restock supplies, and key exchange. Price varies according to location and size of apartment.

- www.Handy.com: Cleaning and handyman services on a per hour basis, with a minimum booking of 2 hours. Full price is based on the number of hours selected. Up to 24 hours before booking you can cancel and reschedule for free. Also good for furniture assembly (think

IKEA!), moving help, interior painting, faucets, and light fixtures. In selected cities in US, Canada and UK.

- www.Proprly.com: Cleaning and key delivery services for Airbnb® hosts and homeowners using Airbnb®, HomeAway, and VRBO. Services include laundry, key delivery, cleaning, restocking supplies, and welcome gifts. Currently available in Manhattan and Brooklyn, NY.

- www.BeyondPricing.com: Assists you by means of an algorithm for optimal pricing. Uses a formula to price the home, evaluates nearby similar listings to help price your home competitively. Calculates local demand for each night by modeling hotel prices, flight data, conference attendance, and more. Preview recommended prices after analyzing the health of the listing, the neighborhood, and local demand. Activate the automatic pricing with one click and the prices are updated on a daily basis. By pricing properly for demand surges, you help capture last minute bookings to earn more each month.

- www.PillowHomes.com: PillowHomes takes command of your listing and for this you are charged a monthly fee, whether they rent it out or not. This service is presently in selected neighborhoods in San Francisco and Los Angeles.

- www.GuestHop.com Check in and concierge services for guests using home sharing websites like Airbnb® and VRBO.

- www.MyVRhost.com One stop vacation rental service in San Francisco.

- www.Maidthis.com Provides professional cleaning services for hosts in Los Angeles and Orange Counties.

- www.MyUrbanBnB.com Short term management for urban home sharing in Boston.

- www.GuestPrep.com Started by hosts for hosts and offers high quality cleaning that fits the "Cleaning Fee", operating in Washington D.C., Austin, Texas and coming soon to Denver, Nashville, Miami, and NewYork.

- www.BoxBee.com Storage solutions company serving San Francisco, Oakland, and Berkley. Delivers easy to pack boxes and stores securely until needed.

- www.Lockitron.com: Unlock your door using Bluetooth low energy technology and any IOS and Android phone.

- www.Skybell.com: Answer the door with a smartphone and the smart video doorbell allows you to see, hear, and speak to each visitor at your door whether you are at home or away.

- www.Concur.com: Using it with TripLink simplifies the booking experience for business travel and helps organizations reduce costs. Travel and expense data is recorded using the app in conjunction with Airbnb®. To enroll, the company must use TripLink, then go to Airbnb® in the Concur App center. Log onto your existing Airbnb® account and click the option to expense through Concur.

Other home-stay companies:

- www.HomeAway.com
- www.HomeStay.com
- www.VRBO.com
- www.Evolvevacationrental.com
- www.VegVisits.com

It is recommended to cast your net wide once you have gotten your Airbnb® listing up and going. Optimize you space and be on at least two channels to open up to as much demand as possible!

Invite Friends to use Airbnb® or become hosts through your Airbnb® page. Each guest who does so will receive a $25 discount on their first booking and the host will receive $25 travel credit. If others become a host, you will also receive a $100 travel credit towards your own future travel.

Chapter 11 - Lessons Learned

Wow! This is the most difficult chapter to write, as the lessons are still coming in on an almost daily basis!

There have been many joys of being a host, and one of them is reading the many kind and glowing reviews. Making even a small difference in someone's life is very heart-warming.

If you thought this was about making money, you will be pleasantly surprised to learn that this business is also about connection and caring.

In going over the almost 50 reviews we have thus far received, there are four common threads, and none of them have to do with money! Almost all the reviews vowed they would return here again on the next trip to the Los Angeles area, and a few have done that!

Most mentioned in the reviews were our amenities and attention to detail. Stocking the fridge with drinks, a bottle of wine, and jar of chocolates got a lot of raves. Also, having plenty of towels, toiletries, and a few robes in the closet!

Second most mentioned in the reviews was the immaculate cleanliness.

The third was the feeling of being welcomed, cared about, and our friendliness. We take a real interest in the reason for our guests' visit and give suggestions and assistance when asked.

The last was feeling as if they were in the own home or staying with family, in comfort and security. Add these all together and they equal a personal experience not available in any corporate hotel chain.

One guest told us our place was amazing and she felt completely welcome.

She said: We were here for a wedding, and I was supposed to be getting a dress delivered from UPS. It never showed up, and UPS said they wouldn't be able to deliver it until Monday, two days AFTER the wedding. Roxanne offered to let me see the dresses she had to see if I wanted to borrow one. She made it one of the best trips I have ever taken—I'd 100% recommend staying here!"

Just asking her one question: *Do you want to borrow a dress from my daughter? She is about your size and she has a few dresses you may like;*

made a huge difference in my guest's experience!

The most memorable guest was a young man from Baltimore here for a photo shoot in Hollywood.

He writes *"Words cannot describe the level of hospitality provided. The house was beautiful, very clean, organized and everything you can expect. My trip took an unexpected turn of events and I ended up in an auto accident. They came and picked up my friend and I from the hospital, made sure we were okay and checked up on us every day. I felt like she was my mom! "*

"This was an above and beyond business experience and I feel like I have gained more from my trip to LA due to meeting this family. Words cannot fully describe the gratitude I have and whenever I am traveling to LA this is the place where I will stay."

Of course we picked them up and took care of them—that's what we do!

I was just recently speaking with a guest who told me she felt such love and care in the apartment; she wanted to take photos of the sayings and pictures on the walls to remind her of the weekend! She also said she felt spoiled as we thought of everything she could want during her stay and that we felt like family!

That is the "GET" from being a host that warms my heart, as well as the promise to come back and see us.

We had a family from Germany with a baby who was spending her first birthday in America. We made her a giant vegan cupcake and her parents were so surprised when we sang "Happy Birthday" and the baby started laughing. She had not been feeling well their entire trip and the giggling was so healing.

For 5 weeks while their home was covered in volcanic ashes, we were able to care for a family evacuated from the Big Island of Hawaii. Because we control the calendar for our Airbnb® listing, I was able to block off the time so they could stay with us. It is a blessing to help others and provide a roof over their heads.

We have had several first time Airbnb® users as guests. All were surprised at the welcome and how fun it was to stay with us. Others mentioned our apartment is one of the cleanest and nicest Airbnb®s they had experienced and it is now their home away from home.

Whatever your reason, being an active participant in the new sharing economy is reaping rewards—seen and yet unseen.

We wrote this guide to help others with their personal and financial abundance as we have so been blessed.

Special Discounts and Deals for Readers of

"Welcome! A Personal Guide to Hosting Airbnb®"

We are constantly researching and obtaining premiums, discounts, and special offers for our readers.

Please check our web site at
<u>www.WelcomeAirbnb.com</u>
for the latest updates.